W9-ADN-450

DISCARD

LIFE CYCLES
Deer

by Robin Nelson

first step nonfiction

Lerner Publications Company · Minneapolis

Look at the deer.

R0430448957

This deer has **antlers**.

3

Deer are **mammals**, like dogs and people.

How do deer grow?

Baby deer grow inside their mothers.

Baby deer are born in the spring.

Baby deer are called **fawns**.

Most fawns have brown **fur** with white spots.

Fawns can walk soon after
they are born.

But they hide until they can
keep up with their mothers.

Fawns drink milk from their mothers.

The fawn grows bigger.

Now it is a deer.

Young deer eat plants.

Deer live with their family in the **forest**.

It is fun to watch deer grow.

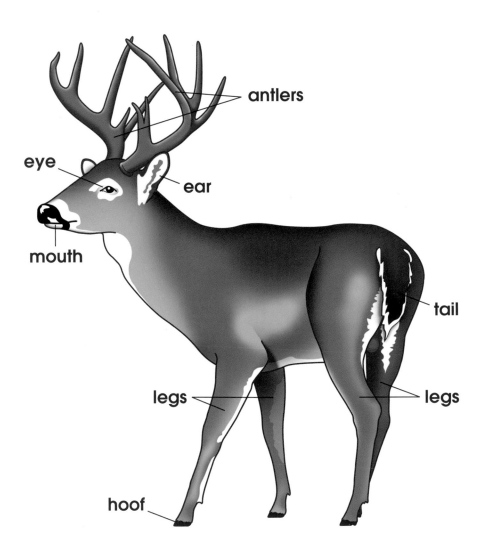

antlers

eye

ear

mouth

tail

legs

legs

hoof

Adult Deer

Adult deer have long legs with hooves. Their long legs help them to run very fast. Only male deer have antlers. The antlers grow in the spring and fall off in the winter.

Smaller deer sometimes live in warmer places like deserts. Large deer live in colder places. Most deer live in forests all year. In the spring, deer get ready to have babies and begin the deer life cycle again.

Deer Facts

 A female deer is called a doe, and a male deer is called a buck.

 Male deer are usually larger than female deer.

 Many deer raise their tail to show the white side to warn other deer of danger.

 The moose is the largest member of the deer family.

 Deer only have front teeth on the bottom of their mouth.

 Wolves, coyotes, cougars, and tigers hunt deer. Sometimes people hunt deer too.

 Deer can be found on all continents except Australia and Antarctica.

 Deer are the only animals that have antlers.

Glossary

 antlers – hard growths on a deer's head

 fawns – baby deer

 forest – many trees growing together

 fur – thick, soft hair covering an animal's body

 mammals – warm-blooded animals that give birth to their young

Index

Copyright © 2009 by Lerner Publishing Group, Inc.

All rights reserved. International copyright secured. No part of this book may be reproduced, stored in a retrieval system, or transmitted in any form or by any means—electronic, mechanical, photocopying, recording, or otherwise—without the prior written permission of Lerner Publishing Group, Inc., except for the inclusion of brief quotations in an acknowledged review.

The images in this book are used with the permission of: © iStockphoto.com/David H. Lewis, p. 2; © Tom Brakefield/Stockbyte/Getty Images, p. 3; © iStockphoto.com/Eileen Hart, p. 4; © iStockphoto.com/Thomas Gordon, p. 5; © Liquid Light/Alamy, p. 6; © Adam Jones/Visuals Unlimited, Inc., p. 7; © age fotostock/SuperStock, pp. 8, 9; © Gerry Lemmo, pp. 10, 13, 16; © Dave Willman-Fotolia.com, p. 11; © Rolf Nussbaumer/naturepl.com, p. 12; © © Wild Geese-Fotolia.com, p. 14; © Tom and Pat Leeson, p. 15; © iStockphoto.com/Eric Naud, p. 17; © Laura Westlund/Independent Picture Service, pp. 18, 20, 21.
Cover: © Tom Brakefield/Digital Vision/Getty Images.

Lerner Publications Company
A division of Lerner Publishing Group, Inc.
241 First Avenue North
Minneapolis, MN 55401 U.S.A.

Website address: www.lernerbooks.com

Library of Congress Cataloging-in-Publication Data

Nelson, Robin, 1971–
    Deer / by Robin Nelson.
        p.   cm. — (First step nonfiction. Animal life cycles)
    Includes index.
    ISBN 978–0–7613–4067–6 (lib. bdg. : alk. paper)
    1. Deer—Juvenile literature. I. Title.
QL737.U55N455 2009
599.65—dc22   2008025709

Manufactured in the United States of America
1 2 3 4 5 6 – DP – 14 13 12 11 10 09